WHAT'S IT LIKE TO BE A . . ?

ZOO KEEPER

Elizabeth Dowen   Lisa Thompson

First published in the UK 2010 by
A & C Black Publishing Ltd
36 Soho Square
London
W1D 3QY
www.acblack.com

Copyright © 2009 Blake Publishing
Published 2009 by Blake Education Pty Ltd, Australia

ISBN: 978-1-4081-2874-9

Written by Lisa Thompson and Elizabeth Dowen
Publisher: Katy Pike
Series Editor: Eve Tonelli
Cover Design: Terry Woodley
Designer: Rob Mancini and Clifford Hayes
Printed and bound in China by Leo Paper Products.

Cover image © Rex Features/Mark Habben

All inside images © Shutterstock except p4 (bl), p7 (mfr), p18 (tl), (tr), p20
(b), p21 (mr), (ml), p24 (tr), p26 (m), p38 (b) – Taronga and Western Plains
Zoos, Australia

With grateful thanks to Taronga and Western Plains Zoos for their generous
support and assistance.

This book is produced using paper made from wood grown in managed,
sustainable forests. It is natural, renewable and recyclable. The logging and
manufacturing processes conform to the environmental regulations of the
country of origin.

All the Internet addresses given in this book were correct at the time of
going to press. The author and publishers regret any inconvenience caused
if addresses have changed or sites have ceased to exist, but can accept no
responsibility for any such changes.

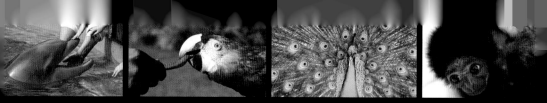

Contents

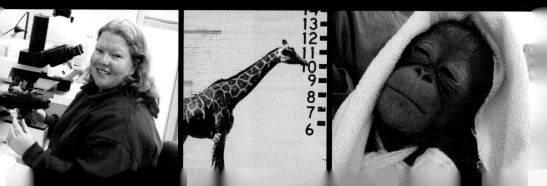

Feeding time at the zoo

The zoo is alive with bird calls and the yawns of lions, gorillas and hippos waking up as I begin my shift as a zoo keeper. My first job is to check on the animals in my area. I make sure I look in on a little koala called Kaya. She has been losing weight and eating poorly for the past few weeks and I am not sure why.

We have been keeping a special eye on her, recording her weight, movement, feeding and sleeping patterns. Today, the vet will examine Kaya to try to find out what's wrong and how we can help her.

Kaya the koala

The other animals look well, so I grab my cleaning gear — wheelbarrow, shovel, rake, broom, mop, hose and disinfectant sprays — and get stuck into cleaning out the animal enclosures. All the enclosures need to be sprayed, scrubbed and dry-mopped during the day. I change the water in each enclosure as well.

all my cleaning gear

The animals know that after cleaning, it's breakfast time — so they're very excited to see me.

As usual, I am pleased to see them too, but this morning I am a little distracted. My mind is on the zoo tour I am leading this afternoon, and I can't help thinking about Kaya and her mysterious lack of appetite. I will feel better when the vet has checked her over.

healthy breakfasts for everyone

Suddenly, I hear people shouting and pointing skyward. I look up to see that Ralph, our wedge-tailed eagle, has escaped and is circling above. As I watch the eagle, his handler uses a special whistle and tempting bait to call him back. Ralph was raised here in the zoo, so I don't like his chances of surviving outside. I wonder how he got out?

What does a zoo keeper or animal carer do?

Zoo keepers look after the animals in a zoo whilst other keepers work with animals in safari and wildlife parks. In a big zoo or park, a group of keepers looks after one kind of animal, such as the big cats or the monkeys. In smaller parks or zoos, keepers can be in charge of a section covering a variety of animals. Keepers clean out the enclosures, feed the animals and keep them happy and healthy.

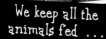

We keep all the animals fed ...

healthy ...

and their enclosures clean.

Where do animal carers work?

Caring for animals in captivity is not limited to zoos. Animal carers also work at wildlife parks, aquariums, theme parks, mobile animal displays, animal rescue centres and bird collections. There are about 350 such places in the UK run by zoological societies, charitable trusts, local authorities or private businesses. They employ around 3,000 people.

aquariums

In wildlife parks, where animals live in conditions similar to the wild, keepers have less contact with them, but observe their behaviour and routines. Zoo keepers must also be excellent observers and be able to detect subtle changes in an animal's physical or psychological condition.

Zoo keepers and animal carers have many different tasks to do every day, such as:

✓ • prepare food for the animals
• order and collect special foods such as gum leaves for koalas, and crabs for the blue-ringed octopuses

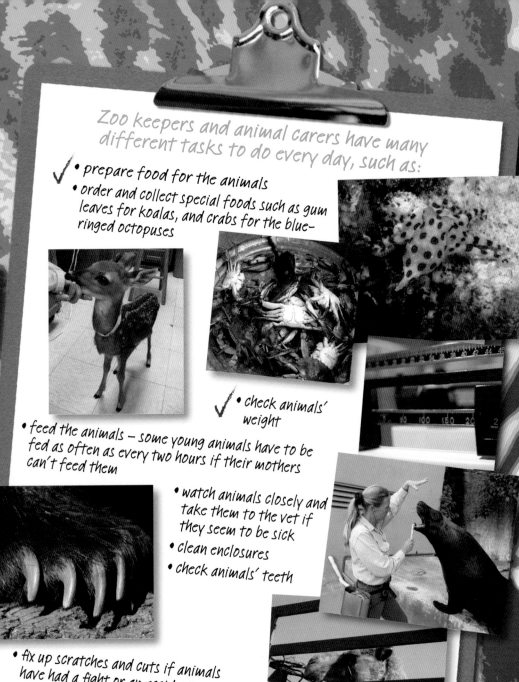

✓ • check animals' weight

• feed the animals – some young animals have to be fed as often as every two hours if their mothers can't feed them

• watch animals closely and take them to the vet if they seem to be sick
• clean enclosures
• check animals' teeth

• fix up scratches and cuts if animals have had a fight or an accident
• check feet or hoofs of animals such as giraffes and elephants
• clip long nails
✓ • give talks to the public about the animals

• move animals to new enclosures or into night yards
• travel with animals on trucks, ships or planes when transferred to other zoos

7

Timetable of my typical day

7:30 am Animal check — look for any abnormal behaviour, illness or injury. Often if an animal is sick, it will show signs of illness in the morning.
–Prepare and serve morning feed.
–Clean outdoor enclosures.

✓ **9 am** Move animals to their outdoor exhibit areas for opening time.
–Clean indoor holding areas.

12:30–1:30 pm Lunchtime.

1:30 pm Prepare afternoon feed and order food for following morning.

3 pm Do weigh-ins and general health check of animals.
–Write daily reports for each animal.

✓ **5 pm** Move animals back to indoor/sleeping areas.
–Serve afternoon feed.
–Observe animals for any sign of sickness or injury.

5:30 pm Lock up enclosures before leaving.

preparing feeds

coming outside for the day

doing health checks

✓ Where do the animals live?

Each animal has its own special needs for shade, shelter, vegetation, water features and landscaping. So, animal keepers look after all kinds of enclosures – from aviaries (both walk-through and closed-off), paddocks and aquariums, to cages and habitat boxes.

👁 Keep your eyes on that eagle

We discovered a hole in the mesh of the aviary, allowing the eagle to escape. Who knows how that happened? It may have been nibbled by one of the animals who walk the park freely.

I leave the hole open for now and put out a feed of chicken and fresh water. You never know, Ralph may just return to his enclosure by himself.

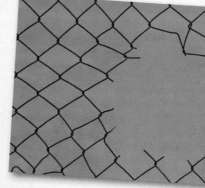

Meanwhile, the birds of prey keepers try to follow Ralph, but it doesn't take long before they lose sight of him. They drive around hoping to spot him, but see nothing. We alert the local vets, in case he is brought in injured. All we can do now is wait.

Growing up, I always loved animals. My family had a dog, a cat and a fish, but I was always collecting other animals and looking after them. Big or little, it didn't matter. I collected ants, bugs, butterflies and lizards. I also had a rabbit, a parrot and a duck. I was fascinated by each animal's behaviour and finding out how best to take care of them.

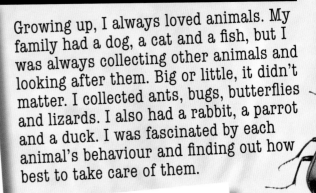

Binky

Mr Chuckles

Oscar

I loved having lots of pets at home.

Every school holiday, we would visit an animal park or zoo. We all had our favourite animals we wanted to see. My older brother liked the giraffes, while my little sister thought the pandas were cool. I loved seeing the chimpanzees.

When I was 14, I got a volunteer job at an animal shelter. That job was a good start, but I wanted to work with many different animals when I got older. So I applied to be a volunteer at a local animal park. I was rejected quite a few times but I finally got accepted. My persistence paid off!

I got my first real experience at the shelter, looking after unwanted and lost pets.

I stayed as a volunteer at the park right through school and then enrolled in a NPTC Advanced National Diploma in Animal Management at college. That was great, because I could see what I was learning being put to use when I was working at the park. I was keen and up for anything when I was volunteering. I wanted experience with all the animals.

When I finished my studies, I used my experience and qualifications to get a full-time job working at a zoo. Now I have the experience it's my job to look after all sorts of exotic animals.

The emus at the animal park were hard work, but I enjoyed it.

DIDYOUKNOW?

Giraffe tall tales

- Giraffes are the tallest land animals in the world, growing up to 6 m tall. Like us, they have only seven neck bones – but a giraffe's are much longer!
- No two giraffes have the same pattern of spots.
- Their blue-black tongues are up to 53 cm long!

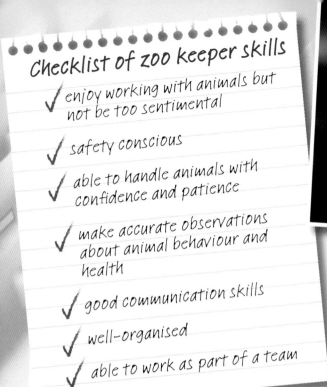

Checklist of zoo keeper skills

- ✓ enjoy working with animals but not be too sentimental
- ✓ safety conscious
- ✓ able to handle animals with confidence and patience
- ✓ make accurate observations about animal behaviour and health
- ✓ good communication skills
- ✓ well-organised
- ✓ able to work as part of a team

Cool or scary? I say cool!

Paperwork has to be done too.

Caring for animals is a great job because you never stop learning. Because you become attached to the animals, it can be sad when they die. But it can also be very exciting — when there is a birth, for example or watching the animals grow and become adults.

Loki — our new baby tiger!

The job has a lot of responsibility. The animals rely on you for food, shelter and sometimes comfort too. Their health and happiness is your priority, but it's a job that gives you a lot back — and you never know what's going to happen next!

Crystal, with her mum, Snowy

Do you have what it takes?

Looking after animals means being physically active and on your feet. You will work outdoors in all kinds of weather and conditions may be wet, cold, dirty, muddy, smelly, hot or humid. The work is physically demanding and you will probably lift or carry heavy loads. Keepers work at least 40 hours a week. They work on a rota basis to ensure that every day of the year is covered.

A big part of becoming a zoo keeper or animal keeper is getting hands-on experience. Volunteer jobs or traineeships will give you a chance to handle and look after animals.

Try getting work at:
✓ pet shops
✓ farms
✓ pet breeders
✓ animal shelters
✓ veterinary surgeries
✓ animal welfare organisations
✓ wildlife parks

pet shops

animal farms

animal shelter

Saving wild animals

Red squirrels

My local WILDLIFE TRUST in Northumberland wanted a volunteer conservation assistant to help the 'Save our Red Squirrels' project. I applied and got the job in my holidays! My main role was to help in wildlife survey, follow up sightings and help in the office keeping the information up-to-date.

We need information about red squirrels to decide exactly why the population has declined so much and work out ways in which we can help them recover. We may be able to provide extra food to help them over bad winters or breed them in captivity and re-introduce some into protected, suitable habitats.

DIDYOUKNOW?

Wild, eh?

The Wildlife Trusts' movement is the largest voluntary organisation working in the UK on all aspects of nature conservation. The 47 local Wildlife Trusts across the whole of the UK, the Isle of Man and Alderney, have 765,000 members.

Why are red squirrels endangered?

Until the 1940s there were loads of red squirrels in the UK. But now they have disappeared from many areas and their place has been taken by the grey squirrel. Grey squirrels put on a lot more body fat than red squirrels which gives them a better chance of surviving.

Grey squirrel

The grey squirrel is more adaptable than the red squirrel and lives in hedgerow trees, parks and gardens as well as large woods and forests. Grey squirrels are also immune to the squirrelpox virus, which is deadly to red squirrels.

Endangered animals

Long-eared owl

Wildlife conservation isn't just about Africa or the Amazon. These British natives need your help, too:

Scottish wildcat
Long-eared owl
Bumblebees
Marsh Fritillary (Butterfly)

Spiny seahorse
Water Vole
Common Skate
Leatherback Turtle

DID YOU KNOW?

Dead as a dodo

The dodo has become a symbol of extinction. It was a turkey-sized flightless pigeon which lived on the island of Mauritius until 1681. The extinction of at least 500 species of animals has been caused by man, most of them in this century. Today there are about 5,000 endangered animals and at least one species dies out every year.

The eagle is sighted!

Around lunchtime, a local resident calls to say he has spotted a wedge-tailed eagle in a tree near his house. Two keepers take nets, gloves, a transport box and Ralph's favourite food (chicken) to entice him back to safety.

On first sighting, the feathers standing up on the back of his neck tell them Ralph is scared and tired. Since he has never been out of the zoo before, Ralph doesn't know how to find water or food, so he is probably thirsty and hungry.

In the past, Ralph would be rewarded with chicken if he landed on his keeper's glove. One of the keepers decides to try it.

The keeper puts on the glove to protect his hand and arm from the eagle's sharp talons, and holds out a piece of chicken. The zoo keeper stands statue still. Suddenly, there is a whoosh from the bushes and Ralph swoops down. In the split second he is on the glove, and the keeper has captured him with the net — success! Ralph is then put carefully in the transport box.

Back at the park, the enclosure is repaired while the vet checks Ralph over. He gets the all clear, so Ralph is returned to the safety of his enclosure.

Go Maggie, go!
Elephant gets treadmill

In 2005, the Alaska Zoo in Anchorage had what was believed to be the world's first elephant treadmill. Maggie the elephant tipped the scales at 4132kg – about 450kg overweight. Zoo director, Ted Edwards said he hoped the elephant could learn to use the treadmill to lose her extra kilos.

'Every time we've taught Maggie something new, she has always learnt it faster than we expected,' Mr Edwards said.

Zoo officials said one of the challenges facing captive elephants was making sure they exercised through Alaska's long winters. But when the overweight pachyderm turned up her trunk at jogging, she was loaded on an Air Force C-17 and flown to northern California. Maggie's departure followed years of debate over whether she should leave Alaska for a warmer part of the country where she could exercise and be around other elephants.

Why do we have zoos, aquariums and wildlife parks?

Zoos, wildlife parks and aquariums educate people about mammals, birds, fish, reptiles and amphibians in their natural environments. People see them up close — and can smell, hear and sometimes even touch them.

Signs provide information about where each species comes from and how it lives. Keepers and guides give talks so people understand the animals better.

This keeper is doing a bird show for our zoo visitors.

This touch table lets visitors find out what animal skin feels like.

The role of zoos and animal parks has changed over time and they are now involved in conservation. There is work that is carried out in the field and conservation breeding programmes.

Field-based conservation

The Zoological Society of London (London Zoo and Whipsnade), Marwell, Bristol, Jersey, Paignton, Newquay, Living Coasts and Edinburgh, all specialise in conservation of animals in their own habitat. They can focus on any species from bats, to whales or insects, in the UK or abroad.

Tasmanian devils are under threat from a facial tumour disease. Zoos may play an important part in ensuring their survival.

Breeding programmes

Zoos and parks breed species in captive settings. Several species like the Arabian and scimitar-horned oryx and Przewalski's horse, which became extinct in the wild in the 20th century, have been bred in captivity and returned to the wild.

These people, on safari in Africa, are lucky enough to see animals in the wild.

The first drive-through safari park outside of Africa opened in 1966 at Longleat in Wiltshire England. The idea of safari parks came from Jimmy Chipperfield, co-director of Chipperfield's Circus. There are now safari parks in most regions of the UK.

DIDYOUKNOW?

Zoo history

The Egyptian queen Hatshepsut, sent out the first recorded animal collecting expedition in the 15th century BC. The expedition sailed down the Red Sea coast of Africa and brought back a variety of animals. Roaring lions, monkeys and even a giraffe crowded the decks as slaves rowed the tiny boats back to Egypt.

In ancient Greece, zoos were a display of wealth and knowledge, and were the hobby of private citizens.

In the 4th century BC, the great Greek philosopher and scholar Aristotle owned an experimental zoo of monkeys and birds. He carefully observed and recorded their behaviour and was able to describe 300 species in his great book *History of the Animals*.

Queen Hatshepsut

The Greeks wanted to learn about animals.

19

Working in a zoo or wildlife park community

Lots of people work in zoos and wildlife parks to make sure the animals are happy and healthy, and visitors have a good time. Here are some of the jobs.

Director/ Park manager

Every zoo or park has a director or park manager who is in charge. They work with the government and other zoos and parks, in the UK and internationally, in their conservation and research work. They plan for the future and decide the types of animals kept at the zoo. They also oversee the running of the zoo itself.

Veterinary team

Vets check the animals regularly so they stay healthy. A vet nurse assists the vet. A zoo or wildlife park vet has to be prepared for all kinds of problems – from an iguana with a sore eye to a hippo with a tummy ache. Vets may also need to operate on very sick animals.

Research officer

Some zoos and parks have research departments where zoologists help co-ordinate research and conservation projects.

Education officer and assistant

In the biggest parks and zoos this includes teaching sessions, delivering presentations and lectures, animal outreach to surrounding schools and groups, fundraising for conservation campaigns and running summer schools/activities.

Horticultural (gardening) staff

The gardening staff have the big job of keeping all the grounds healthy and attractive. They may have to understand the plant life of the desert, savannah, forest, tropics and even the aquarium to ensure animals are happy in their habitat. Some staff may also specialise in maintaining botanical gardens.

Trade division

Some animals need artificial lights, heating or air conditioning to stay alive. Carpenters, painters, electricians and plumbers must keep everything in good working order.

Administration and retail team

There are also staff working in finance, IT, Human Resources, marketing, fundraising, catering, visitor services and retail.

Volunteers

Many people are happy to volunteer to work with the animals. You usually have to be 18 and be willing to do all kinds of tasks.

Eat this!

My most important responsibility is feeding each animal a balanced diet. We prepare most food in a specially designed area. As much as possible, we feed the animals exactly what they would eat in the wild.

Vitamins and special pellets or cubes are sometimes added. These are made from chaff with dairy products or protein added. Apes, marsupials and hoofed animals love them. Seals are fed fish with vitamins hidden in the gills.

All the necessary nutrients are in here.

It doesn't take long for an animal to work out if food contains a vitamin or a medicine if it doesn't taste quite right. It's up to me to get creative in the kitchen and think of new ways to get the vitamins and medicine down.

Hiding these tablets is no easy job.

DIDYOUKNOW?

Toes and noses

Tapirs have 14 toes (4 on each front foot and 3 on each back one) and can move their flexible noses in all directions to smell – especially if there are bananas about!

Open wide! ✓

Is your camel no longer taking vitamins or medicine wrapped in bread? Try drilling holes in carrots and hiding them inside – one bite and they're gone!

Who eats what? ✓

When it comes to food, all animals fall into one of the following categories:

- **omnivores** – eat meat and plants
- **carnivores** – eat meat
- **herbivores** – eat plants
- **insectivores** – eat insects

Where is it?

Keepers will hide food from the animals and encourage them to look for it. This method, known as enrichment, stimulates the animals to behave as they do in the wild. An animal can spend up to half an hour working to find its food and will enjoy it even more.

Grizzly bears are omnivores (so are we).

Food games

To encourage natural behaviour and keeping them from getting bored, food doesn't just come on a plate! It can be thrown onto a roof, pulled through a mesh, cut very small so that it can be scattered, hidden in boxes or paper sacks.

Tapirs are only into their grass and plants.

Zoo Menu

Zoos and wildlife parks develop their own food mixtures to match the tastes and nutritional needs of their animals. Some animals' appetites also vary from season to season. Keepers know food must be interesting to the animals and given in the correct amounts, so they spend lots of time weighing, chopping and preparing food to get it just right.

Animal	Food Intake (each adult per day)
Condor	2 rats (or 10 chicks)
Wedge-tailed eagle	1 rat
Elephant	90 kg hay
	2 loaves of bread
	bucket of carrots
	dairy meal cubes
Giraffe	1 bucket carrots
	1 bucket pellets
	bale lucerne
	2 branches gum leaves
	dairy meal cubes
Kangaroo	kangaroo pellets (protein supplement)
	lucerne
	3–5 carrots
	vegetation (trees, grass, etc.)

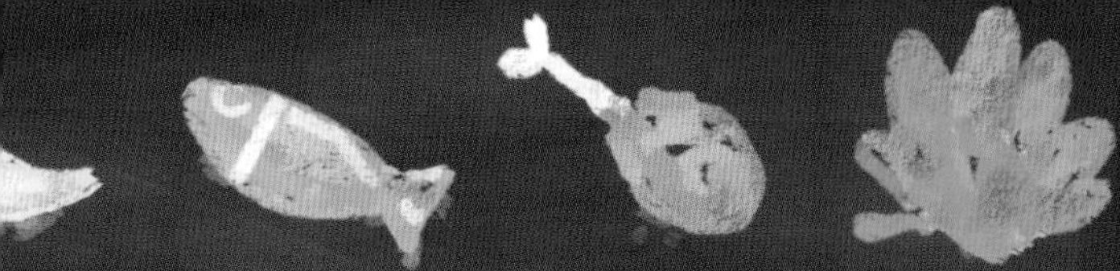

Food Intake (each adult per day)

15 kg carcass (usually beef or horsemeat)

10 kg mince for males, 7 kg for females

1 chicken

bones

mixed chopped fruit and vegetables

eggs

boiled chicken

2-5 cups skim milk

(diet varies according to size of snake)

2 mice per week

7-8 rats per week plus 1 rabbit every 3-4 weeks

2 teaspoons fly pupae

4 tablespoons mixed fruit and vegetables

crumbed dog kibble

1 protein cube

native flowers

mealworms

Food for thought

Animals can develop health problems if given the wrong food. Tortoises' shells may go soft and flamingos can lose their colour. Koalas will starve themselves to death if they are not fed the correct types of eucalyptus leaves. Penguins can get sick without enough salt in their diet.

DIDYOUKNOW?

Hmmm ... yummy

Zoos and wildlife parks often breed their own food, such as grasshoppers, cockroaches, flies, mealworms, locusts, earthworms, rats and mice, to feed to other animals. However, apart from invertebrates such as worms, no live animals are fed to zoo or park animals.

The frozen zoo

San Diego's CRES (Centre for Reproduction of Endangered Species) has an incredible resource called the Frozen Zoo. Scientists there collect cells from animals by taking a small notch of ear or skin during a routine vet visit. They then grow cell cultures of the animals' DNA in their laboratory and freeze them.

He's just putting some antelope cells into these dishes.

These samples are used to study genetic variation in populations of animals such as the gorilla, rhinoceros, bonobo and dikdik.

If only we'd had this technology before the dodo disappeared!

Scientists hope the frozen cells will help explain genetic problems. If an endangered animal's living cells are in the Frozen Zoo, they may be able to be used to prevent the extinction of the species.

✓ What is a dikdik?

A dikdik is a tiny antelope. It has a dainty appearance and is slightly larger than a hare.

the dikdik

Rhinos and bonobos could benefit from this kind of research.

Monkey Business

Thirty chimpanzees escaped from their enclosure at a zoo in Cheshire, forcing it to be closed in July 2009. The animals found their way into a nearby keepers' area, where their food is usually prepared. How the animals got out is not known but they were not in an area accessed by the public. Chimpanzees are thought to be the most intelligent non-human primate.

London Zoo

London Zoo was opened in 1826 when Sir Stamford Raffles founded the Zoological Society of London. The Zoo had a number of 'celebrity' animals over the years including:

- a hippopotamus called Obaysch, often visited by Queen Victoria

- Winnie, an exceptionally tame bear who gave A.A. Milne the inspiration for Winnie-the-Pooh's name

- Chi-Chi, the Giant panda, who refused to breed but instead made advances to the famous zoologist, Desmond Morris!

Animal lover extraordinaire

The amazing hero of the
mountain gorillas — **Dian Fossey**

Dian Fossey was an animal behaviourist who
began studying endangered African mountain
gorillas in 1967. Observing and recording their
behaviour, her work took her to Zaire and then
to Rwanda — where she opened the Karisoke
Research Centre.

After years of Dian's patient observation, the gorillas
knew and trusted her, and she could sit in the
midst of a group and even play with their babies.
Eventually, she could recognise individual animals
and even gave them names.

The gorillas were in constant danger from poachers.
Dian campaigned against poaching and went on
a quest to tell the world about the extraordinary
gorilla. This made her very unpopular with poachers.
In 1985, she was found murdered in her cabin. Her
killer has never been found.

Dian Fossey's work with the mountain gorillas means
that while they are still endangered, they are now
protected. If she had not brought the plight of the gorillas
to the world's attention, they might be already extinct.

MURAKAZA NEZA
MU RWANDA
BIENVENUE AU
RWANDA
WELCOME TO
RWANDA

Here's a silverback —
an adult male gorilla.

DID YOU KNOW?

Sad but true
There are fewer than
650 mountain gorillas
left in the world.

a mountain gorilla

29

How exciting

The zoo is expanding its crocodile exhibit, and the zoo director has just told me that I will be in the study team. We will be going to northern Australia for two weeks to study crocodiles in their natural habitat.

I will also study other native reptiles that we may bring back. Studying animals in their natural environment helps zoos better care for animals in captivity. It's also a very adventurous and exciting part of the job!

We need to learn how to feed them properly ...

and how to breed them too.

✓ Hey stinky, are you the boss?

Meerkats work out who the head female and male are in their group by who has the strongest scent. With meerkats in captivity, keepers spray their enclosure with patchouli oil and other fragrances to confuse the animals for the first few weeks the group is together. This gives them time to settle in before they work out who is the boss.

DID YOU KNOW?

Animal counting!

Each year staff at London Zoo have to do a stock-take of every animal. The zoo's huge population – 14,567 animals at the last count – means it takes keepers about a week to complete. Among the new additions this year are the first lion cubs born there in a decade, a pair of nosey aardvarks and a Komodo dragon.

Group names

A group of meerkats, containing 5–30 members, is called a mob or a gang. Some other animal group names (collective nouns) include:

- a troop of baboons
- a leap of leopards
- an ambush of tigers
- an ugly of walruses
- a zeal of zebras
- a murder of crows

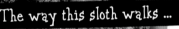

The way this sloth walks ...

Let's talk

Most keepers form a strong bond with their animals. The animals learn to trust and understand the routine of the environment and their keepers. Although they never speak the same language, a keeper can often tell what an animal is thinking and feeling by:

✓ the way they walk

✓ the way they stand

✓ the look on their face

✓ the sounds they make

✓ the condition of their fur or feathers.

the way this lioness looks ...

and the condition of this lemur's fur all tell keepers how their animals are doing.

Chimp talk

Read my face ... what am I thinking?

Wild chimpanzees live in large communities of 15–120 individuals and communicate with one another through a complex and subtle system of vocalisations, facial expressions, body postures and gestures.

Speaking chimpanzee

Like humans, chimps say a lot with their faces. You'll be amazed how much chimp-speak you already understand when you take a closer look.

When chimps are angry, they open their mouths wide and show their teeth. They frown and their eyes get smaller just like ours do. They can also make their hair stand on end.

angry chimp

Face 2

When chimps are bored, they look like us when we're bored!

bored chimp

Face 3

When chimps are surprised and interested they open their eyes wide and drop their lower jaw, just like us.

surprised chimp

Face 4

When chimps are happy and feeling playful, they make laughing noises. Their eyes get narrower and they show their bottom teeth. It's a chimp grin!

happy chimp

✓ Aping around

Fifty years ago, there were around a million wild chimpanzees in Africa. Today, chimpanzees are an endangered species with as few as 150,000 left in the wild.

Our future could be happy and secure if our habitat was protected.

AFRICA

DIDYOUKNOW?

Chimp facts

- The chimpanzees' closest relative is us! We share 98.6% of our DNA.
- Chimps can live for more than 50 years.
- Chimpanzees don't like to be in water and usually can't swim.
- Chimpanzees are apes, not monkeys.
- Other apes include gorillas, orang-outangs, bonobos and gibbons.

Kaya gets weighed

Once I have delivered breakfast and cleaned all the enclosures, I take Kaya the koala from her enclosure to the weighing room and pull out her observation folder. I place Kaya in the weighing bucket. She has been going in it since she was a baby, so she doesn't find it strange.

She has lost another 200g. I bundle her up and grab her folder, which outlines her previous weigh-ins, what she is eating and how she has been behaving. It's time to see the vet.

Kaya in her enclosure

Off to the vet

I take Kaya to Eric, the vet. Kaya is unsure of this new, strange environment. She clings to my jumper. I stroke her back and avoid any sudden movements, which would upset her more. I put her gently on the observation table as Eric gives her a look over and goes through her chart.

Kaya's not going to like this, but Eric will be gentle with her.

Eric thinks that Kaya may have had a tick that put her off her food. She has a lump behind her left ear where the tick might have been, but there is no sign of it now.

I wonder if this little bug has made Kaya sick.

Eric has to run some tests to find out what's wrong.

He looks in Kaya's ears and all over her body. There are no signs of scratches, bites or other ticks. Eric takes a blood sample for testing. We decide that Kaya will stay in the zoo hospital until she starts improving and putting weight back on.

Kaya checks out her new surroundings.

The tour

Leading tours and talking to visitors is a part of the job but I had to get used to it. I am much better with animals than people! Even so, it is very rewarding. My groups get to find out how amazing animals really are.

Meet our friend, Freddie the parrot.

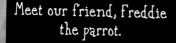

Tours are a chance to get up close!

She's already met Kylie the cockatoo!

We walk past the hippos and stop to admire our new arrival — Lizzie, the baby hippopotamus. I explain that hippos ooze pink goo to keep their skin from drying out when they leave the water. So, Lizzie's gooey skin is actually the sign of a happy, healthy hippo baby.

We watch as Lizzie takes a drink from her mum. Baby hippos are fed by their mothers until they are about eight months old. They stay close to mum until they are about two or three years old.

Lizzie and her mum.

Then we go into the Wild Animal Care Centre, and watch as a keeper feeds a baby raccoon with a bottle.

This baby, Rocky, is being raised by a keeper after his mum stopped paying attention to him when he became sick. When Rocky gets bigger and stronger, he will be reintroduced to his raccoon family again.

Rocky getting his lunch

Bob takes over the rest of the tour.

We pass the wedge-tailed eagle enclosure and I tell the group about the great eagle escape. Then it's time to hand the group over to the next keeper.

With my part of the tour done, I begin to think about Kaya again. I'll pay her a visit after I finish my daily animal reports.

I wonder how Kaya's doing?

✓ Writing animal reports is very important.

Kaya's progress

The vet gives Kaya different eucalyptus leaves to try. Koalas are picky eaters and out of 800 species of eucalyptus, they may only like the taste of 40. Kaya begins to munch on some blue gum leaves, but stops after a few bites. Time to try some other leaves.

The next day

Kaya's blood sample comes back normal, so there's no answer there as to why she is losing weight. The mystery remains. The vet decides to feed her a batch of good quality peppermint gum leaves, a variety she has never tasted before, and guess what – she eats the lot!

Next few days

Great news! Kaya's appetite is returning to normal and she's slowly gaining weight. She is chomping down peppermint and red gum leaves – definitely on the road to recovery. It might have been a tick bite that put her off her food, although the vet thinks Kaya might also have a case of the fussy eaters.

Eric brings in a fresh supply of eucalyptus leaves for Kaya.

Just like people, animals get sick of eating the same thing all the time. Now that Kaya loves peppermint gum leaves, she'll be back with the other koalas by the end of the week.

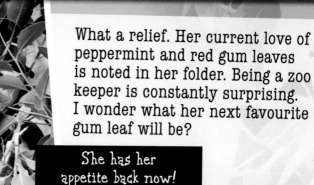

What a relief. Her current love of peppermint and red gum leaves is noted in her folder. Being a zoo keeper is constantly surprising. I wonder what her next favourite gum leaf will be?

She has her appetite back now!

DIDYOUKNOW?

Just eating and sleeping

Koalas rest for up to 20 hours a day and spend most of that time asleep!

They eat half a kilo of eucalyptus leaves every day and live nearly all of their lives in trees.

Practise being an animal keeper now!

You can start developing important animal keeper skills right now.

Record keeping

This is something keepers do every day. In a notebook, make daily notes of anything you think is important about your pet. Write down what you see, hear and smell. Your notes will help you if your pet gets sick. Look at things like:

- **health**
- **weight**
- **behaviour**
- **diet**
- **training**

Make notes about:

✓ how your pets move — quick, energetic, stiff, limping?

✓ how well they eat — quickly, carefully? Favourite foods?

✓ how their fur, feathers, skin or scales look — dull, dirty, clean, shiny or smooth?

Know what they need

Keepers need to create a comfortable, relaxing yet interesting environment, where an animal will behave naturally.

Look for things they like to eat and have in their environment. Do research to find out how the animal lives in the wild and what conditions best suit them.

He looks comfortable to me.

research

Watch their diet

Animals need fresh, healthy food to eat and you must know what can make them sick.

Always keep food and water clean, and save treats for special occasions. Watch how much your animals eat – you don't want them getting too fat or too skinny.

Remember you can also tell a lot about an animal by their droppings and urine.

Clean up!

It is a keeper's job to keep the animals' areas clean and fresh. Get a nose that can handle cleaning up animal waste.

Treats are not an everyday food.

Volunteers needed

Volunteering is the best way of gaining experience. This can be:

✓ dog walking and kennel duties

✓ looking after injured animals

✓ working at local community farms

✓ monitoring local wildlife

✓ working with stray and feral cats

✓ riding for the disabled groups

✓ working for the NSPCC or other animal charities

Follow these steps to become a keeper

Step 1

To start you off you will need three to five GCSEs (grades A*-C) or the equivalent, some specifying English, maths and biology.

Step 2

Use your work experience placement to gain more experience. Try to get a placement at a zoo, animal park, farm or vets. Any other hands-on placement would be worthwhile. Make sure the placement you choose shows you have commitment and put as much time in to it as you can. A part-time job would also be helpful.

Step 3

After school, there are a number of animal-related college courses to consider including:

- the Diploma in environmental and land-based studies at Levels 1 to 3, and in animal care and management at Level 4
- NPTC Level 2 National Certificate in animal care
- Foundation Modern Apprenticeship in animal care.

Step 4

Some zoos and parks require higher qualifications, such as A/S levels (Biology), a BTEC National Award, Certificate or Diploma in animal management or an NPTC Advanced National Diploma in animal management.

Step 5

Often trainee keepers have HNDs, degrees in subjects such as animal management or zoology.

For more details ask your Connexions PA, careers adviser or teacher.

Red-hot fact!

People working with animals can be very well qualified, even up to PhD level. There are about 3,000 keepers in the UK and it's highly competitive!

Key tips

As well as the exams and work experience or volunteering these other skills are useful:

✓ **Get yourself a driving license.** It is often asked for in advertisements for keepers, particularly by smaller zoos.

✓ **Learn to drive a tractor.** This is something many keepers have to do as part of their daily work.

✓ **Learn First Aid.** Any attraction visited by the public needs a first aider, someone accredited by the Red Cross or St John's Ambulance in the First Aid at work course.

✓ Read **articles and magazines** on current animal issues and keep up to date on developments in animal care.

✓ Be familiar with **computers and software packages**. Records of animals are often kept on a computer system called ARKS (Animal Record Keeping System) so a daily report sheet must be filled in by each keeper to update this database.

✓ Take a look at the **short term courses** advertised by zoos or other animal organisations.

✓ Many of the larger zoos and parks will take on **temporary employees** during the summer.

Money facts

Starting salaries are around £10,500 per year and experienced keepers earn about £17,000. A head keeper may earn up to £24,000.

Opportunities for zoo keepers

In larger zoos, there may be prospects of promotion to senior keeper and eventually to head keeper. Finding work with more responsibilities may mean moving to another zoo. There may be opportunities to work abroad.

Other related areas

Veterinary surgeon and nurse

at the vet's

Becoming a vet or vet nurse is a highly popular career choice. A vet is responsible for the prevention of disease and for the medical and surgical treatment of animals including domestic pets, zoo animals, wildlife, farm animals and horses. Veterinary nurses help veterinary surgeons (vets) treat and look after sick and injured animals. You can qualify as a veterinary nurse in two ways – work-based training or higher education.

Zoologist

Zoologists work in a wide range of job areas that involve studying animals and their behaviour, including development and testing of new drugs, conservation of endangered habitats and species and animal welfare.

Marine biologist

Marine biologists research the sea, its life forms and surrounding coastal areas. They analyse the oceans and their interaction with the land, atmosphere and sea floors, and their areas of study could include anything from microscopic bacteria to the largest whales.

Animal carer

There are many other jobs working with animals from stable work, working in a pet shop, dog grooming, and farming, to animal rescue work.

Wildlife conservationist

Wildlife conservation officers can include managing habitats, environmental impact assessments, and field surveys. They work for a large range of charities such as the Wildlife Trust, or the RSPB.

Useful contacts

Zoos UK www.zoosuk.zookeepers.co.uk
A directory of all zoos and animals parks in the UK.

Association of British Wild Animal Keepers (ABWAK)
www.abwak.co.uk
A fabulous resource for all kinds of information related to this career.

British and Irish Association of Zoos and Aquariums (BIAZA)
www.biaza.org.uk
The professional body representing the best zoos and aquariums in Britain and Ireland. It has very useful *directory of available animal courses in the UK*. Regents Park, London NW1 4RY Tel: 020 7449 6351

Zoological Society of London www.zsl.org

NPTC www.nptc.org.uk
NPTC offers animal management courses.

The Wildlife Trust UK www.wildlifetrusts.org
The largest UK voluntary organisation dedicated to conserving the full range of the UK's habitats and species.

RSPB www.rspb.org.uk
The RSPB works to secure a healthy environment for birds and all wildlife.

Short Courses
The Jersey Wildlife Preservation Trust runs a Summer School or a Certificate in Endangered Species Management. Similar courses are run by Edinburgh Zoo.

Jobs
Jobs and volunteering opportunities may be advertised on individual zoos' websites, in Cage and Aviary Birds and on the websites of the British and Irish Association of Zoos and Aquariums and the Association of British Wild Animal Keepers.

Glossary

animal behaviourist – scientist who studies the behaviour patterns of animals

cell culture – cells from plants or animals grown in a laboratory under controlled conditions

chaff – outside part of grain; used as animal food

DNA – deoxyribonucleic acid – found in the cells of all living things; passes on characteristics from parents to children

enclosure – area surrounded by any kind of fence or wall

enrichment – to make better; add quality to make more enjoyable

extinct – died out; none left of a species due to hunting, environment changes or natural causes

extraordinaire – exceptionally outstanding

genetic – relating to the genes (DNA) of a living thing

habitat – where an animal lives

humane society – charity that campaigns to protect wild animals and stop cruelty against all animals

humanised – when an animal becomes accustomed to humans and human contact

invertebrate – animal without a backbone

nutrient – anything taken in or eaten by living things

poacher – person who illegally kills protected animals for food or for money

pupa – insect at the stage of changing from baby (larva) to adult, e.g. caterpillar in its cocoon before it becomes a butterfly

rehabilitate – to restore to a natural condition; make well or better again

vocalisation – sound made to communicate, eg grunting, talking, singing

Index

other titles in the series

PILOT

FORENSIC SCIENTIST

TV PRODUCER

MAGAZINE EDITOR

GAME DEVELOPER

MOTOR MECHANIC

ANIMATOR

BUILDER

CHEF

SPORTS TRAINER

FASHION DESIGNER

CHOREOGRAPHER

FIRE FIGHTER

MARINE BIOLOGIST

LAWYER